AI Prompts for Everyday People -

By: Troy Evans

Table of Contents

Introduction

This world of artificial intelligence (AI) can seem pretty daunting, especially if you are not a tech savvy person. As a person born in the '70s, I get it 100%. When I first started diving into AI platforms like ChatGPT and Gemini, I felt a bit lost and frustrated. Even after being a tech engineer and business owner for 20 years, from the '90s into the 2000s, I still could not wrap my mind around the practical use of this tool that had everybody excited. I just could not find a way to integrate it into my everyday life. I could not find a real way to make my life more productive, so I didn't.

Before I knew it, I morphed into an end user/consumer who was extremely skeptical. In 2022, I was landing the plane on my second career as a Pastor and had no interest in learning anything else. So, like many people, I downloaded ChatGPT and asked a few weird questions, got bored, and left it alone for months. I made a picture and turned classic songs into rap songs. Though it was very fun, it was not sustainable. My time is extremely valuable to me; making Willie Nelson do a rap song was not the most productive use of my time.

Then, I saw a random short video on YouTube that gave me a different perspective on the practical use of AI platforms. I do not remember exactly what was said but I was challenged not to be the old, out-of-touch dude because I'm really not that type of person.

I'm typically in tune and cutting edge. I'm the crazy man who started a Hip Hop church called The EDGE.

But with AI, I feel like I am becoming the person who works my nerves, the old guy who goes on and on about music that the youth are listening to but never picks up the music and listens to find out what's under the hood.

And when pressed to explain why they don't like the music, they give broad and often half-baked answers. This was me... I became what irritates me the most: a closed-minded person when it comes to AI. So, I decided to invest in the paid version of ChatGPT. I started researching what AI is and what its use cases are in life, business, and ministry.

I committed to learning one thing a day for three months about AI, large learning, and deep learning models. At times, it was foggy, and I felt as if I was studying for nothing. It was a new world of terminology that I was not familiar with. There are not a lot of people who have the practical expertise to answer my questions.

So, YouTube University and I spent a significant amount of time over what became six months. Though I am not where I want to be in my understanding or remembering all the terminology, I was able to make sense of it and learn something about this amazing tool literally every day!

More importantly, I was able to reconcile why I would invest my most valuable commodity (time) into this technology. Since then, my approach to everyday tasks for business, fun, and study has been flipped upside down. AI has become a major part of my family, ministry, and business life.

I used to use ChatGPT once every few weeks, but now I'm using it 20 times a day on average. What I learned is that seeing AI as more than another app to download vs. a tool that can be leveraged to maximize my productivity helped me to realize that if understood at even a basic level, I could regain 20% of my life.

I could be 20% ahead of my competitors in the marketplace. I can be 20% more knowledgeable. I can be 20% more efficient. This compound reality makes a compelling case for the use of AI. I will say that my overall productivity has increased by 2X. Who wouldn't want to be more productive?

In the next season that I was entering, I needed to multitask while ensuring that the quality of my work stayed intact. I calculated that I spent, on average, 7 hours per day studying, listening, and or using AI-powered tools or materials for 6 months. Literally refraining from learning anything else. That's a lot of time spent on one subject.

What I learned was that the foundation of an everyday person actually using AI to be more productive lies in getting proficient at what's called **prompt**

engineering. It sounds technical, and on the back end, it gets extremely complex and high-level tech.

Thankfully, companies like OpenAI and Google thought this tool should be in the hands of not only engineers, techies, and developers but also everyday people for everyday use.

I am 52 years old at the time of writing this book, and I have found myself surrounded by leaders who are a bit older than I am. It has been pretty dope to see these leaders take my training, read my materials, utilize my free AI resources, and integrate AI platforms into their everyday leadership and lives. Seeing the light come on has been absolutely amazing.

On a really personal note, AI has restored my love for words by helping me get better at reading and writing. When I picked up the basics of what AI is and how I might use it in my everyday life. I started by writing a book with my daughter. This was a heartfelt project because both my daughter and I struggled with reading as kids. She went on to complete her education and became a teacher/reading specialist.

In my own case, I failed the 7th grade three times and did not really learn to read decently until in my 20s. But even then, I struggled for years reading and writing. I published a book many years ago with the help of a ghostwriter, Anne Byle. I would not have ever completed a book if it were not for the genius and patience of Anne.

Even back then, before high-speed internet was poppin', I would record my stories one chapter at a time, and she would step in and make it all make sense. I decided to learn AI by having it take my recorded notes and sermons and transcribe them, then put them through ChatGpt and GEMINI to help me make sense of it all.

Now, 6 months later, I've released 7 books, including this one, and let me tell you... **Having AI as an assistant has leveled the playing field** and is allowing me to produce the books I always wanted. I've had many thoughts until now I never had a way to be engaged in the process as my more educated counterparts.

I can't help but think about kids in school who struggle with math and reading like Toni, and I can now have tutors at their disposal. Or the elderly person who can't put the words together like they used to but they are not done thinking and producing content. When understood and carefully executed, this technology can provide life and hope to so many people. It did for me. Join me on this journey as I take you on a ride to the world of AI and its many benefits.

Chapter 1

What is AI?

AI is a word that has been thrown around alot lately. I mean, you can't go to social media and the news without hearing about artificial intelligence. This is why it's crucial to have a basic understanding of what AI actually is so that you know what AI is not. We often use the term AI in a very broad sense, but we can break it down into three main categories:

1. Artificial Intelligence (AI)

2. Machine Learning (ML)

3. Deep Learning (DL)

Artificial Intelligence (AI) is basically a machine doing human-like stuff. Think of it as a robot or software that emulates human intelligence, like recognizing faces in photos or understanding spoken language.

Machine Learning (ML) is a subset of AI. Basically, it's when machines learn from data and improve their performance over time without a human telling them what to do. Imagine teaching a dog to go get a stick. At first, it might not get it right, but with practice and rewards, it learns exactly what you want it to do.

Deep Learning (DL) is a more advanced form of Machine Learning. It uses complex structures called neural networks, which are inspired by how our brains work. Deep Learning can process and learn from large amounts of data to perform very specific tasks, like translating languages or recognizing objects in images and more.

AI is a tool that helps people work smarter, faster, more efficient, and not harder.

I really think it's critical that you understand these differences at some level. Here are a few everyday examples. This will help you understand how to identify and interact with AI.

- **AI**: Have you ever talked to Siri or Alexa before? When you ask them to play your favorite song or set a timer, that's AI at work. They understand what you're saying and respond appropriately, just like a helpful assistant.

- **Machine Learning**: When Netflix suggests movies you might like, that's Machine Learning! It looks at what you've watched before and learns your preferences to suggest new shows and movies that fit your taste.

- **Deep Learning**: When you upload a photo to Facebook, it automatically tags your friends; this happens because of Deep Learning. The software has learned from millions of images to recognize faces and understand who is in each picture. This is to tell you that AI has been in existence for a long time. Let's take a dive into the history of AI from its inception till date.

The History of AI

Though platforms like ChatGpt hit the scene in the 2020^s, AI has been around for decades. The roots of AI can be traced back to the 1950s when a group of scientists and mathematicians, including Alan Turing and John McCarthy, started exploring the idea of machines that could think and learn like humans.

- **The 1950s**: Alan Turing proposed the Turing Test, which is a way to see if a machine can exhibit intelligent behavior that is equivalent to that of a human. If you can't tell the difference between a machine and a human in conversation, then the machine has passed the test!

- **The 1960s-70s**: During this time, researchers developed the first AI programs that could solve problems and play games like chess. These programs laid the groundwork for future AI technologies.

- **The 1980s-90s**: Interest in AI waned for a while, but then it experienced a resurgence thanks to advances in computing power and the availability of large datasets. This period saw the development of Machine Learning, which allowed computers to learn from data instead of being programmed with every single rule.

- **The 2000s-Present**: Today, AI is booming! With the explosion of the internet and access to vast amounts of data, AI technologies have become more sophisticated. Companies like Google, Amazon, and Facebook are using AI to enhance user experiences, analyze data, and improve their services.

AI is Everywhere, and it Ain't going nowhere!

AI is woven into our daily lives more than we realize. Every time you use your phone, shop online, or even get recommendations for what to watch on TV, you're interacting with AI. In 2024, **77% of currently used devices feature some form of AI.** 25% of travel and hospitality companies use chatbot technology. 64% of business owners believe AI will boost productivity.

(AI Statistics: The Present and Future of AI 2024 Stats)

One common misconception is that AI will take over jobs and replace humans. While it's true that AI can automate some tasks, it also creates new jobs and opportunities. It is also true that AI will take jobs. However, according to experts, X-Eyee is the senior policy advisor for the <u>Goldman School of Public Policy at UC Berkeley</u> and the CEO of <u>Malo Santo,</u> an AI consulting firm. **Jobs will be taken, but mostly by people who have learned, adapted, and figured out how to utilize AI responsibly in the workplace.** I'll ask you as you read further not to think of AI as the mysterious creatures destined to replace humans. We will look at this misconceptions in detail in the last chapter of this book. Think of AI as a tool, an assistant that helps people work smarter, faster, more efficient, and not harder. Bottom line... AI isn't going anywhere; in fact, it's only going to become more integrated into our lives. The key is understanding how to use it safely and effectively. Just like learning to ride a bike or use a new app, mastering AI is about practice and getting comfortable with the technology.

So, in short, AI is a fascinating and powerful tool that mimics human intelligence, while Machine Learning and Deep Learning are specific ways that AI learns and improves. Understanding these concepts will help you navigate the growing world of AI and make the most of what it has to offer. As we dive deeper into this book, we'll explore how to communicate effectively with AI and create useful prompts. By the end, you'll be equipped to see the value of using AI every day and its potential to enhance your personal life and work.

I can't say this enough: **This eBook is designed for everyday people, not tech experts.** We'll use simple language, relatable examples, and analogies to make sure you understand exactly how to work with AI assistants like they're your own personal assistants.

AI isn't going anywhere; in fact, it's only going to become more integrated into our lives.

Whether you need help with meal planning, car shopping, or even creative writing, solid AI prompts are the keys to unlocking a world of possibilities. Trust me, once you see how AI can make life easier, you'll wonder why you waited so long to explore these amazing tools.

We'll use straightforward language, real examples, and lots of analogies to help you understand how to work with AI assistants. We will take one step at a time, and by the end of this book, you will have enough knowledge about using tools like ChatGPT & Gemini and the like.

DO THE RIGHT THING

Let me quote the great scholar Ben Parker—yeah, Spider-Man's Uncle... **"With great power comes great responsibility."** It's so important that we use

AI responsibly and ethically. It's all about finding that sweet spot where we can use AI and all of its greatness for a good while, staying away from any craziness that comes with this power. I think understanding the difference between AI-assisted and AI-generated stuff will be helpful in our attempt to do the right thing.

Utilizing AI correctly is called AI-assisted. This is like having a ridiculously smart assistant who knows everything that has ever been written. This assistant can help with your writing, suggest new ideas, or even help you work through a difficult conflict. **It's all about a collaboration between you and the AI, where you remain in the driver's seat the whole time.**

AI-generated content, on the other hand, is like the AI doing a solo performance. It creates stuff all on its own, which is pretty cool, but it also raises a lot of questions. Like, who's the real creator? Is the content original? And ultimately, who's in control / in the driver's seat? This book and every book I authored is a collaboration between my Assistant AI and me. **The key word here is assistant.** I come up with the concept and then start writing. I hit up my assistants and give them what I'm thinking. They help me get to the next phase of my process. Then, I flush out my ideas and use assistants like Google Gemini to help me along the way by flushing out the rest of my ideas, refining the text, and making it even better than I could on my own. We do this ping-ponging literally dozens of times in a single book writing process.

It is said that a 200-page book can contain around 50,000 to 60,000 words. So, if a person could write 40 words per minute non-stop, they could have the first draft done in about 24 hours of sustained writing. Well, though it is probably *humanly* possible to stay up for 24 hours and knock it out, it's probably not the norm or advised.

So, let's say it's realistically 60 hours for a human; with AI, you can truly get a finished product completed within that 24 hours, stretched over however many days you need. **Using AI can redeem valuable time doing mundane things so that you can stay in the creative space.** But I'll say this again: the key to all this is the human commitment and discipline of staying in the driver's seat at all times while receiving assistance along the way.

It is also important to note that AI has the tendency to hallucinate or make stuff up. So, when using it as a research tool, it is important that you fact-check and source the facts. The latest models of AI platforms like ChatGpt and Gemini now have web search integration, which means they can confirm data in real time in your text window. It is still important that you cross-reference the "facts" that AI provides.

Recap

Artificial Intelligence (AI) is becoming a big part of our everyday lives, so understanding its basics is essential. AI is a broad term that can be divided into three categories: Artificial Intelligence, Machine Learning, and Deep Learning. AI is like having a helpful assistant that can understand and respond to human requests. Machine Learning, a branch of AI, allows machines to learn from data and make predictions without human instructions—think of Netflix learning what you like to watch. Deep Learning goes even deeper, using complex neural networks to recognize faces in photos or translate languages.

AI has been developing since the 1950s, evolving from simple problem-solving programs to today's sophisticated tools used in apps and websites. While AI raises concerns about job loss, it can also create opportunities for those who learn to work with it. The key is to use AI responsibly as an assistant to help, not replace, human effort.

Activity:

1. **Identify AI in Daily Life:** For one day, note each time you interact with AI. It could be your phone's voice assistant, streaming recommendations, or even an online shopping suggestion.
2. **Classify AI Type:** Using the chapter's breakdown, decide if each interaction is AI, Machine Learning, or Deep Learning. Write down your classifications.
3. **Reflection Questions:**

- How did AI simplify or improve your experience?
- Did you feel more in control, or did the AI seem to operate on its own?

Remember, AI is a tool to aid and not replace human potential.

Chapter 2

AI YOUR EXPERT ASSISTANT

AI has quickly become an incredibly useful tool in our daily lives, acting as a knowledgeable assistant that can help with a wide range of tasks. Imagine having a reliable friend who's always ready to answer questions, find information, or even help with planning and organizing. That's essentially what AI is doing for millions of people right now.

This expert assistant role isn't limited to just basic tasks. AI can help in specialized areas like medicine, where it can assist doctors in diagnosing diseases, or in finance, where it supports analysts in spotting trends. It learns from the data it's given, getting smarter and more capable over time. Despite all the complex technology that makes it work, AI has a very simple goal: to make things easier for people, saving time and effort, and often providing insights that might otherwise take hours to discover.

Let's give your assistant a little bit more specific expertise so you can really see what I'm getting at. Imagine that you have your three experts sitting in front of you, each with unique skills and knowledge. One's a culinary genius, another's a car expert, and the third knows random facts about the Bible. Instead of tracking down each expert individually, you've got them all in one place, ready to help you with whatever you need.

That's what AI assistants like ChatGPT are for you. They are your personal team of experts waiting to be put to work. The key is learning how to talk with them, and that's where good prompts come in. The art of creating the perfect request or "prompts" will help you get the results you want. In every AI platform, you have some sort of message/text box where AI is patiently waiting for you to give it its next set of instructions to knock out.

Whenever you're going after a task that requires you to use your device, big or small, there's probably a way AI can look out for you. So, before you start, ask the Golden Question: **"How can my AI Assistants help me get it done?"** This question will be especially helpful as you learn to integrate AI into your daily life and work. Early on, if you don't train yourself to ask yourself this critical question, you will underutilize this powerful tool.

For example, If you're planning a backyard barbecue, instead of flipping through cookbooks or endlessly scrolling online, you can ask your AI assistant for help:

- **You**: "Hey AI, I'm planning a barbecue for about 10 people next Saturday. Can you help me out?"

- **AI**: "Sure thing! First, what kind of vibe are you going for? Casual and laid-back, or something a bit more out there?"

- **You**: "Pretty casual. I want to make great-tasting food on a charcoal grill, but I'm not sure what to serve besides burgers and hot dogs."

- **AI**: "Got it. I can suggest some delicious grilled recipes that go beyond the basics, like marinated chicken skewers, veggie kabobs, or even grilled fruit desserts. I can also help you plan a timeline for prepping and cooking, so you're not stuck at the grill all day. How does that sound?"

- **You**: "That sounds great!"

- **AI**: "I'm glad you like these options. Would you like me to create a barbecue feast that has 3 meats, 3 starches, 2 veggies, and a dessert? Include recipes and instructions on how to smoke the protein."

(PAUSE: Actually open ChatGPT and give this a try)

See how that works? By giving your AI assistant a clear idea of what you need, you get personalized help that saves time and makes your barbecue fire!

AI ASSISTANTS FOR EVERYDAY LIFE

As we explore the power of AI prompts, it's important that you at least know a few of the top platforms available today. From communication assistants to creative tools, these cutting-edge technologies can revolutionize how you approach daily tasks and challenges.

1. **ChatGPT**: This is like having a crazy-smart friend who's good at explaining stuff. You can have real conversations with AI, ask for help, and even work together on projects.

2. **Midjourney**: Ever wished you could paint like a pro? This tool turns your words into pictures! Just describe what you want, and it'll create an image for you.

3. **Claude**: Think of Claude as your helpful assistant who's good at all sorts of things, from research and writing to coding.

4. **Google Gemini** can assist with tasks like content creation, language translation, and answering questions, making it a versatile tool for both personal and professional use.

5. **InstructGPT**: This AI is a pro at following instructions and breaking down big problems into smaller steps.

6. **Church.Tech**: This is a platform where you can start with sermon notes or YouTube links and create amazing content for children's ministry and weekly devotionals.

7. **NotebookLM** is an AI-powered tool that helps you take and organize notes more efficiently. It can summarize information, suggest related topics, and make collaboration easier so you can focus on learning and understanding.

8. **Wave AI Note Taker** is a smart note-taking app that uses AI to capture and organize your notes. It features voice-to-text transcription and automatic summaries, making it simple to find and manage your information while improving your productivity.

There are new platforms dropping every day. When you understand what these platforms can do and learn how to talk to them, your daily tasks and big projects will become much easier to roll out. When you have assistants from AI, you can stick to what you know how to do well, and AI will help with the rest.

WRITE PROMPTS LIKE A BOSS

AI assistants like ChatGPT have the ability to understand real talk, provide in-depth analysis, and even collaborate on detailed projects. But if you are going to get the best bang for your buck out of these tools, it's important to master the art of creating solid prompts.

I've been conducting business for 25 years, all across the US and England. I have been beyond blessed to have had really talented assistants at all levels. The truth is, I suck at most things and could not accomplish all that I do without the help of extremely talented assistants. Due to the complexity of my life, I have needed two assistants on many occasions. Yeah... I'm that messed up.

What I have learned over the years is that **your assistants are only as helpful as you allow them to be, and no matter how skilled they are**, they cannot read your mind. If you were on the phone talking to your three amazing assistants and you wanted them to accomplish something very specific the first time, what would you need to make sure you do when communicating with them? You would need to be very specific.

The more detailed your instructions (prompts) are, the better your AI assistant can tailor the

The more detailed your instructions (prompts) are, the better your AI assistant can tailor the response to your needs. Let's take it a step further. If you meet the most talented assistant, and though they know everything about everything on the internet, they know what you want and how you need it. There is a

24

classic movie with Adam Sandler and Drew Berry Moore called 50 First Dates. Adam meets Drew, and they fall in love the first day they meet. He says good night and goes back to talk to her again, and she has zero clue who he is. He then finds out from her family that she suffers from temporary amnesia. So he goes on a journey to try to remind her every day of who he is while reintroducing himself to her daily. This is Ai in a nutshell. It doesn't remember you, your details, your likes or dislikes without you telling it to. This is where prompting comes into play.

Imagine you're working on a marketing campaign for a new product launch. Instead of a vague request like:

"Give me some ideas for this campaign,"

Try a prompt more like:

"ChatGPT, as an expert in developing marketing campaigns for a new eco-friendly water bottle that filters dirty water into clean drinking water. Can you provide me with 5 unique and attention-grabbing tagline ideas that highlight the product's key benefits?"

(PAUSE: Actually open ChatGPT and give this a try)

By feeding it with specific details about the product, your target audience, and the desired outcome, you're giving ChatGPT the necessary context to know what you want from it and ultimately generating a more useful response. This level of detail not only helps your AI assistant understand your needs but also encourages it to explore more creative and innovative solutions than you would ever be able to come up with yourself.

Of course, the power of prompts doesn't stop at the initial request. The true magic happens when you leverage the power of follow-up questions. After receiving that first set of tagline ideas, you could then ask ChatGPT more.

PROMT: "Can you provide a brief explanation for why you think each of these taglines would be effective in attracting our target audience of eco-conscious millennials?" or "Can you generate 3 additional tagline ideas that incorporate the concept of 'clean water' in a more subtle, aspirational way?"

(PAUSE: Actually open ChatGPT and give this a try)

By digging deeper and asking for more information or other approaches, you are able to engage AI in a back-and-forth dialogue that reminds it of what you're looking for, which leads to better output. But don't be scared to be yourself as you're communicating. While keeping a clear objective, you can add a little sauce to the interaction. This will help AI to get to know you and also allow you to just be you, which always produces better results.

We don't need you to get stuck on words. Just say what you are thinking and press enter. ChatGPT even understands your slang and misspellings, which is extremely helpful for dudes like me. So don't overthink typing it right. Just focus on telling the AI what you need. This type of prompting not only taps into the AI's ability to understand context and role-play but also encourages it to think outside the box, often creating some pretty nice results.

Just like any other skill or tool, the key to mastering AI prompts is practice, practice, and more practice. I think a goal is to be intentional about spending 15 minutes each day asking AI to help you figure out stuff. Then, monitor the results and make adjustments to your request until you find the sweet spot that gives you what you're looking for. Just like in real life, the more you engage with your AI assistants, the better you know how to communicate with them, and the better they'll become at understanding your unique needs and preferences. By regularly engaging with AI with detailed prompts, you'll be well on your way to transforming the way you approach everyday tasks and problem-solving.

WRITE PROMPTS FOR DAILY STUFF

Let's work from another angle with your AI Assistants. Let's imagine you needed to plan a big family dinner. Normally, you'd have to consult a handful of different people like that aunt who's an amazing cook, your neighbor who knows all the latest food trends, and your colleague who's a self-proclaimed grill master. But what if you could pull on all of their expertise with just a few taps on your phone?

That's essentially what you get when you learn to craft effective AI prompts. Instead of tracking down all those individual experts, you've got ChatGPT, your own personal culinary consultant, ready to provide recipes, cooking tips, and even grocery lists tailored to your needs.

And the best part is, you don't have to be a professional chef to get these kinds of results. Just like you'd explain your dinner plans to your aunt in simple terms, you can communicate with ChatGPT using plain language and see how it translates into a gourmet meal plan.

The key is being very specific about what you want. We will go into detail in this simple-to-use framework in just a few pages. But our **REACTO** framework is perfect for helping create a simple language that gets results.

R - Role

E - Example

A - Application

C - Context

T - Tone

O - Output

For example, you could say:

Prompt: "Act as my personal chef with 30 years of experience. I have leftover chicken, broccoli, and rice in the fridge. I need 3 quick and healthy dinner recipes using those ingredients that my whole family will enjoy. Provide the recipes in an easy-to-follow format."

By clearly defining the **Role** (personal chef), providing a relevant **Example** (the ingredients on hand), specifying the **Action** (3 dinner recipes), giving the necessary **Context** (family-friendly, healthy), and indicating the preferred **Tone / Output** (simple, easy-to-follow), ChatGPT will be able to generate personalized meal ideas that fit your needs perfectly.

(PAUSE: Actually open ChatGPT and give this a try)

You can use this same approach for all sorts of everyday tasks like researching the best-used car to buy, getting assistance on your next book, or even coding a custom app. Yes, you heard me... if you can explain it, you can build it in code. I started with a 4 simple sentence idea and built it into a full-blown invention with schematics and code. The opportunities are endless!!

Let's jump back to that family dinner scenario. Imagine you're on the phone with your aunt, trying to explain what you need help with. You wouldn't just say, "Hey Aunt May, I need some recipes." You'd give her context about the ingredients you have, the dietary needs of your family, and maybe even your preferred cooking methods. That level of detail is what allows her to provide you with truly useful recommendations. AI prompts work the same way. The more information you can provide, the better the AI assistant can tailor its response.

Recap

In this chapter, we explore the power of AI as a personal assistant capable of managing both simple and complex tasks. From answering questions to organizing projects, AI can support us in various ways. This chapter illustrates how effective AI assistance comes from giving clear and detailed prompts, enabling the AI to better understand our needs and deliver more useful, personalized responses. With practice, writing these prompts can become second nature, turning AI into an invaluable daily resource.

The chapter also introduces the REACTO framework, a strategy for creating structured prompts that specify Role, Example, Application, Context, Tone, and Output. This approach helps users fine-tune their requests and unlock AI's full potential across tasks, like planning a meal, strategizing marketing campaigns, or building a custom app. The key takeaway is that the more information and clarity we provide, the better AI can assist, making it a powerful tool in both personal and professional settings.

Activity:

1. **Scenario Setup**: Open an AI platform like ChatGPT.
2. **Prompting Practice**: Use REACTO to create a structured prompt for an AI-generated solution. For instance, "Act as a travel planner; I need a 3-day itinerary for New York City, focusing on budget-friendly activities."
3. **Refine**: Experiment by adding more context or follow-up questions to enhance the AI's responses.
4. **Reflect**: Assess how changes in your prompts affect the quality of responses, gaining insight into effective, prompt engineering.

Chapter 3

R.E.A.C.T FRAMEWORK

You are on your way to being an official AI whisperer! In order for us to take your prompting to the next level, it is critical that you master this simple yet powerful prompting framework. It will ensure you get the results you are looking for and become the backbone for all you do in AI platforms.

The **R.E.A.C.T. framework** is your secret weapon for crafting clear, effective prompts that get you the results from the AI assistant you want. Let's break down each part of REACT so you can start using it like a pro and unlock the full potential of AI assistants in your everyday life.

The REACT framework consists of the following elements:

R - Role:

Provide a clear description of the persona or expertise you want the AI to embody. This could be a job title, industry expert, or specific point-of-view. Be as specific as possible to set the right context. If the person is famous enough, you can even use their name.

- **Example 1**: "You are Mother Taressa, and you are advising someone who's responsible for planning and executing events to engage local youth and families in their community."

- **Example 2**: "You are an expert in community engagement in urban communities with 30 years of experience, responsible for planning and executing events to engage local youth and families in their community."

E - Example:

Include a relevant example, framework, or template that the AI can use as a guide for structuring its response. This could be a sample plan, report, or even a link to an external resource. This is like casting the right actor for a movie. By telling the AI to "act as a fitness trainer" or "a history buff," you're setting the stage for the kind of response you want. It's like giving your AI a specific hat to wear, helping it focus its expertise. Think of this as showing, not just telling. Giving an example is like providing a sample of what you're after. If you want a poem, show the AI a poem you like. This helps the AI understand your style and expectations, leading to a more tailored result.

- **Example**: "Review the attached 3-month outreach event plan template used by other successful community organizations as an example framework."

A - Action:

State the specific task, request, or objective you want your assistant to accomplish. Use clear verbs to communicate what you want. This is your clear instruction, like telling your assistant exactly what you need help with. Be direct and specific – "Write a blog post," "create a meal plan," and "summarize this article." This guides the AI's efforts and ensures you get the output you're looking for.

The R.E.A.C.T. framework is your secret weapon for crafting clear, effective prompts that get you the results from the AI assistant you want.

- **Example**: "Create a detailed 3-month rollout plan for the urban ministry's upcoming community outreach event targeting local kids and families."

(PAUSE: Actually open ChatGPT and give this a try)

C - Context:

Provide relevant background information and user details to give the AI the context to create a good response. This is the background info, the extra details that fill in the gaps. It's like giving someone the whole story, not just a snippet. Context helps your assistants understand the details of your request, leading to a more relevant and helpful response.

- **Example**: "The urban ministry wants to host an interactive event to build relationships and provide resources for underprivileged youth in the surrounding low-income neighborhood. The goal is to increase attendance and participation from the community over the 3-month period."

(PAUSE: Actually open ChatGPT and give this a try)

T - Tone:

Indicate the appropriate language style, mood, and level of formality you want the AI to use in its response. This sets the mood, like choosing the right music for a scene. Do you want a formal report or a friendly chat? Specifying the tone helps the AI match your desired style, making the interaction feel more natural and engaging.

- **Example**: "Present the plan in a professional yet approachable tone, as if you are pitching the strategy to the ministry's leadership team."

(PAUSE: Actually open ChatGPT and give this a try)

Exercise to Work on 15 Minutes EVERY DAY for 7 Days Straight:

Remember the Golden Question: "Can AI help me with this?"

1. **Choose a Task or Project**: Decide on a task or project you'd like to tackle with the help of an AI assistant (e.g., brainstorming marketing ideas, conducting research, or generating creative content).

2. **Apply the REACT Framework**: Craft a prompt that addresses your specific needs using the REACT framework:

   - **Role**: What role or persona do you want the AI to assume?

   - **Relevant Examples**: Provide relevant details, examples, or context about your task or project.

   - **Action**: Clearly specify the desired action or outcome you want the AI to perform.

   - **Context**: Offer additional context and details to further guide the AI's response.

   - **Tone**: Indicate the preferred tone or style you'd like the AI to adopt.

3. **Refine Your Prompt**: Based on the feedback received, refine your prompt and then submit it to the AI.

4. **Analyze the AI's Response**: Evaluate the effectiveness of your prompt. Consider how you could further refine it to achieve even better results.

Remember, the key to mastering AI prompts is practice and continuous refinement. By regularly engaging with this exercise, you'll develop the skills and confidence to elevate your productivity, creativity, and problem-solving abilities through the power of AI assistants.

R.E.A.C.T CHEAT KEY

- **R: Role** - Clearly define the persona or expertise you want the AI to embody.

- **E: Example** - Providing a relevant example, framework, or template to guide the AI.

- **A: Action** - Stating the specific task, request, or objective you want the AI to accomplish.

- **C: Context** - Giving the AI the necessary background information and situational factors.

- **T: Tone** - Indicating the appropriate language style, mood, and level of formality you want the AI to use.

Remember, the key is to be intentional with your prompts, continually refine your agents, and always ask yourself, **"Can AI help me with this?"** As you integrate AI more deeply into your life and work, you'll discover new efficiencies, innovations, and opportunities for growth.

Next Level AI Prompts

Recap

In this chapter, we talked about the REACT framework, a practical guide for creating effective AI prompts. This framework breaks down prompt creation into five clear steps: *Role*, *Example*, *Action*, *Context*, and *Tone*. Each step helps shape prompts so that AI can better understand the user's needs, making responses more relevant and tailored.

In REACT, users specify the *Role* the AI should play, like a chef or community expert. *Example* provides AI with a relevant model or framework, guiding its style. *Action* sets a clear goal, telling the AI what to accomplish, while *Context* gives background details for better results. Finally, *Tone* aligns the response style with user expectations. By using REACT, users can maximize AI's potential, allowing it to handle diverse tasks, from content creation to complex problem-solving.

Activity:

1. **Daily Practice (15 Minutes):** For a week, apply the REACT framework to different tasks.
   - **Choose a Task**: Select a daily task you want help with, like content brainstorming or creating summaries.
   - **Craft a REACT Prompt**: Write a prompt using REACT.
   - **Evaluate**: Review the AI's response. Note areas for improvement.
2. **Refine and Repeat**: Adjust your prompt based on feedback to improve results daily.

By regularly practicing, you'll sharpen your prompt-writing skills, empowering you to use AI efficiently.

Chapter 4

From Standard Assistant to Executive Assistant

Back in the day in the tech world, we used to have a term: "From the store to the door." This meant that by the time you bought technology at the store and took it home, it was already considered old. It seems like once the World Wide Web hit the scene, new technology started coming out weekly. Now, it feels like every day, there are hundreds of new tech releases. Platforms like ChatGPT, Google Gemini, and Claude have moved from being tools only techs found useful to becoming major parts of our daily routines. Today, you can't check your socials without being overwhelmed with AI ads.

Even with the influx of readily available technology, many are only scratching the surface of what these AI platforms can truly do. With all of the capabilities of AI, the unknown can be a bit overwhelming, and it's often just easier to avoid the learning curve of another app. But what if we could take AI a step further? What if it's not simply a toy to play with but a next-level assistant in life, work and business, transforming your AI-integrated platforms from a basic helper into an executive superpower that can manage complex projects, aid in brainstorming innovative ideas, and provide solutions that impact your bottom line?

The true power of AI lies not just in its ability to perform simple tasks but in its capacity to learn, adapt, and enhance our capabilities. It's about moving from seeing AI as a novelty to recognizing it as a strategic assistant in our daily lives.

So far, we've embarked on a journey to build a solid foundation with AI as our assistant. Using REACT as a means of effective communication. Now, it's time to unlock AI's executive potential. In this part of the book, we will explore advanced prompting techniques, show you how to build ideas step by step, and demonstrate how to integrate AI in daily troubleshooting and problem-solving.

AI as an Executive Assistant

When you first start using AI, it's important to treat it like a standard assistant. By using this thinking, you learn how helpful AI can be when it comes to productivity. You might ask it to make a menu, write a post or email, or help with a homework problem. This is a great way to get comfortable with AI and integrate it into your daily routine. It's about building the habit and asking that Golden Question. You got it. "Can AI help me with this?" This helps with making it a natural part of your life.

But here's the thing: using AI just for basic tasks is like owning a Bugatti Chiron that drives 250 miles per hour and only driving it around the neighborhood at 25 miles per hour. Never take it out on the open road, where you can push it to its limits safely. You're underutilizing a tool that has so much more under the hood to offer.

In the real world, the best use of an executive assistant is not just to follow instructions you give. A good executive assistant has much more to offer any organization when invited to participate in high-level projects. A true executive assistant is great at anticipating possible threats, managing complex projects, and thinking strategically. They're instinctively proactive, not just reactive. Similarly, AI can be more than a static information system providing basic support.

The true power of AI lies not just in its ability to perform simple tasks but in its capacity to learn, adapt, and enhance

It's a dynamic set of systems working together with you to provide quality solutions one prompt at a time. By engaging with it on a deeper level, you can tap into its ability to analyze data, generate creative ideas, and provide strategic insights. **It's about shifting your mindset from "What can I ask AI to do?" to "How can AI and I collaborate to achieve more?"**

Building Blocks

So, how do you make this shift? It starts with using building blocks. This means taking small, incremental steps that lead to a larger, more robust output. Let's walk through an example to see how this works.

Example: Planning a Fundraising Event

Basic Assistance:

At the basic level, you might ask, "AI, can you help me create a checklist for my fundraising event?" The AI will generate a list of common tasks like booking a venue, sending invitations, and arranging catering. It's helpful, but it's surface-level.

Executive Assistance:

Now, let's elevate the interaction.

- **Planning:**
  - You ask, "You are a expert in Fund Development specializing in Benevon framework. You have successfully hosted 100 profitable fundraising events grossing 100 million in giving. We are organization committed to helping urban youth learn AI. We are based in Michigan and have 290 people in our donor system raiser's edge. We have 1500 followers on Facebook. Based on

successful fundraising events, what unique strategies should we consider for our fundraiser?"

- ○ The AI analyzes data and suggests innovative ideas like virtual reality donor experiences, interactive social media campaigns, or personalized thank-you gifts.

- **Implementation:**

  - ○ You follow up with, "Draft a project plan that includes timelines, key activities, and milestones based on these strategies."

  - ○ The AI provides a detailed plan outlining when tasks should be completed, who might be responsible, and how each activity contributes to your goals.

- **Review and Refine:**

  - ○ You say, "Review our plan and suggest adjustments to improve impact based on donor feedback from previous events."

  - ○ The AI identifies potential areas for improvement, such as enhancing communication or offering more engaging content during the event.

Chain of Thought Prompting

The whole idea of Executive AI-assisted vs standard AI-assisted is determined based on humans and AI interacting back and forth, refining the output with every response from the AI. When engaging with such a powerful tool without building in ethical disciplines early on, a user will be tempted to simply type a prompt and copy and paste. In some cases, that might do the trick and have zero ethical implications. **But there's so much more in store for those who make a commitment to not get lazy.** When fully embracing a process of going back and forth, building with AI assistance is extremely rewarding and worth the time.

Executive AI-assisted thinking is not about getting out of work; it is all about a back-and-forth sharing of concepts, problems, and ideas, allowing the technology to do what it's best at... being an assistant. I'm fully aware that I oversimplified very complex tech. But hey, I'm old and have learned the value of KIS (Keeping it simple).

The simplest way to think of this is the everyday person now has the ability to collaborate and have a real-time dialog with really advanced technology. This collaborative building approach is referred to as **Chain of Thought Prompting (COT)**.

COT uses continuous, evolving prompts that build on each other. Instead of giving the AI a one-off task, you engage in a dialogue, refining and expanding your project through its feedback and suggestions. This "Chain of Thought" helps you dig deeper and get better results. The key to increasing the quality of the output is to break it down into smaller, manageable pieces.

Moving from using AI as a basic assistant to an executive assistant is a significant shift in how you interact with the technology. When we engage with AI as a crucial partner and collaborator, it begins helping us think through complex situations, manage big projects, and come up with creative solutions.

Chain of Thought Prompting involves guiding the AI through a series of connected questions or tasks, building upon each answer to develop a comprehensive solution. It's about creating a conversation where each response informs the next step.

Starting Small and Building Up. Let's say you're interested in writing a story but only have a rough idea. Here is a simple guide on how to go about it.

Step 1: Start Small

You begin with a simple prompt: "You are an expert in writing fiction stories. I want to write a story about a superhero. I am writing kids 8-12 in Mexico. What could be a unique power for my hero?"

Step 2: Build On It

The AI suggests several unique powers. You choose one and ask, "What challenges might a hero with this power face?"

Step 3: Continue Building

After the AI provides potential challenges, you ask, "How could the hero overcome these challenges?"

Step 4: Develop the Plot

You might then say, "Outline a basic plot that incorporates these elements."

By the end of this dialogue, you've gone from a vague idea to a structured plot outline, all through step-by-step collaboration with the AI. That is the complex process of a chain of thought prompting in its simplest form. But the thought applies to even the most complex topics or problems.

Recap

This chapter encourages us to rethink how we use AI. It suggests that, rather than sticking to basic tasks, we should start seeing AI as a high-level executive assistant. Instead of only asking AI for simple tasks like creating a checklist or drafting quick messages, this chapter explores the potential of AI to manage complex projects and assist in strategic thinking. The key lies in taking an incremental approach, or "Chain of Thought Prompting" (COT), where each AI response builds on the previous one, fostering a collaborative flow to develop deeper solutions.

By shifting to this executive-level mindset, we're not just telling AI what to do; we're engaging it as a partner to brainstorm, analyze data, and refine projects based on evolving insights.

The chapter emphasizes starting small, guiding the AI with layered questions, and building up to complete projects. Through exercises like using AI for event planning or story development, the chapter showcases how COT enables more creative and strategic outcomes.

In summary, moving from using AI as a simple helper to a robust executive assistant can elevate productivity, creativity, and problem-solving.

Activity:

Try this exercise:

1. **Choose a Simple Project**: Maybe you want to design a new app or plan a community event.

2. **Start with a Basic Question**: "What are some features that would make a fitness app stand out?"

3. **Use the AI's Answer to Ask the Next Question**: "How can these features be integrated to enhance user engagement?"

4. **Repeat Until You Have a Complete Plan**: Continue building on each response until you have a detailed outline of your project. Be sure to use the REACTO framework to get even better results. This method not only helps you develop your idea but also trains you to think critically and strategically.

Chapter 5

Problem Solving with AI

Conflict can be difficult to navigate, no matter who you are and how long you have been doing it. Even the most skilled leader in conflict resolution struggles with providing comprehensive solutions at times. Conflict is never fun but necessary in everyday life and business. In order to become decent at conflict resolution, a person has to become a master problem solver.

Well, this is a skill that most people haven't taken the time to really understand and execute in a healthy way. Whether in a relationship, raising kids, or a conflict at work, AI can be an assistant that helps you walk through complex conflicts and establish a plan to begin problem-solving.

Again, it's important that you remember you are always in the driver's seat. And being in the driver's seat includes you making the final determination if the advice given to you by your assistant is the most productive. For an extra layer of safety, I would say, after you implement some of these tools I'll mention, send your conflict and the plan you and AI came up with to someone else you trust, allowing them to offer input about your AI-assisted output.

With tools like ChatGPT, you can engage in meaningful discussions about conflicts, problems, or troubleshooting issues. You accomplish this by inviting personas into the discussion to seek their insights based on their individual expertise. I know it's weird... But imagine having a conversation with several experts all at once: a teacher, a scientist, a business executive. Then, they all offer their unique perspectives, next steps, and plans. AI can simulate this by taking on different "personas" all at once in a conversation.

With AI, you are always in the driver's seat. And being in the driver's seat includes you making the final decision if the advice given to you by your assistant is the most productive.

The benefit of AI's Multiple Personas

- **Diverse Perspectives**: Gain insights from various viewpoints without needing multiple people.

- **Simulate Discussions**: Plan projects or debates by engaging different roles.

- **Enhance Creativity**: Explore ideas more deeply by considering multiple angles.

Example

Prompt: "You are now three people: a teacher, a student, and a coach. Let's discuss how to help a struggling student-athlete improve their grades and develop a plan with actionable next steps."

AI Response

- **Teacher**: "I've noticed that your academic performance has declined recently. Balancing sports and studies can be challenging. We should consider implementing a structured study schedule that accommodates both commitments."

- **Coach**: "I agree. Maintaining academic eligibility is crucial. Perhaps we can adjust practice times to allow for dedicated study periods. Additionally, incorporating study sessions into the team's routine could foster a supportive environment."

- **Student**: "I appreciate the support. Managing time between classes, homework, and practice is overwhelming. A clear schedule would help, and having study sessions with teammates might make studying more engaging."

- **Teacher**: "Let's develop a weekly plan outlining class times, practice sessions, and designated study periods. We can also identify subjects where extra help is needed and arrange tutoring if necessary."

- **Coach**: "I'll coordinate with the team to adjust practice schedules and set up group study sessions. Encouraging teammates to participate can create a culture that values both athletics and academics."

- **Student**: "That sounds helpful. Having a structured plan and support from both of you will motivate me to stay on track with my studies while continuing to train effectively."

Next Steps:

- **Teacher**: Create a weekly schedule that includes class times, practice sessions, and study periods.

- **Coach**: Adjust practice times to accommodate study sessions and organize group study sessions for the team.

- **Student**: Follow the new schedule, attend study sessions, and seek help in challenging subjects.

This approach demonstrates how engaging multiple personas in AI can simulate real-life discussions, offering diverse perspectives and fostering comprehensive problem-solving strategies.

Practical Activity: Have a Multi-Person Chat

1. **Choose a Scenario**: Plan a school play or discuss environmental issues.

2. **Define Personas**: For example, a director, an actor, and a set designer.

3. **Start the Conversation**: Prompt the AI to have the personas talk to each other and resolve the problem.

Example Prompt:

"You are three people planning a play: Alex the director, Jamie the actor, and Taylor the set designer. Discuss how to make the play a success and provide next steps."

Human-AI Collaboration in Problem Solving in Various Fields

The world we live in today is filled with complex problems that require innovative solutions. As technology continues to evolve, artificial intelligence (AI) is becoming an increasingly valuable partner in tackling these challenges. Rather than replacing humans, AI has the potential to enhance our problem-solving abilities when we work together. This collaboration between humans and AI can lead to more effective solutions in various fields, from healthcare to business and beyond.

One of the most significant benefits of human-AI collaboration is the ability to process vast amounts of data quickly. Humans are great at creative thinking and understanding context, but we can only analyze so much information at a time. AI, on the other hand, excels at sifting through large datasets to find patterns and trends that may not be immediately obvious. By combining human intuition with AI's data-crunching power, we can discover insights that drive better decision-making.

In healthcare, for example, doctors often face the challenge of diagnosing diseases based on a multitude of symptoms and patient histories. AI can analyze thousands of medical records, imaging data, and research studies in seconds, identifying potential diagnoses that a doctor might overlook. This doesn't mean that AI replaces the doctor's expertise; instead, it acts as a supportive tool, providing valuable information that helps doctors make more informed decisions. This collaborative approach can lead to earlier diagnoses, personalized treatment plans, and ultimately, better patient outcomes.

Let's look at human-AI collaboration in business. Companies are increasingly leveraging AI to improve operations, enhance customer experiences, and drive innovation. For instance, AI can analyze customer data to identify buying patterns and preferences. This allows businesses to tailor their marketing strategies to meet the specific needs of their customers. However, while AI can provide data and insights, it is still up to humans to interpret that information and implement strategies effectively.

AI can also automate repetitive tasks, freeing up employees to focus on more strategic and creative work. For example, customer service chatbots can handle routine inquiries, allowing human agents to tackle more complex issues that require empathy and critical thinking. By combining the efficiency of AI with the human touch, businesses can create a more responsive and satisfying experience for their customers.

In the creative industries, human-AI collaboration is also making waves. Artists, writers, and musicians are experimenting with AI tools to enhance their creative processes. AI can generate ideas, suggest alternatives, or even create original content based on your inputs; you can use my REACTO framework to effectively achieve this. However, the final output often relies on human judgment and creativity.

Education is another domain where human-AI collaboration can make a significant impact. AI-driven tutoring systems can personalize learning experiences for students by assessing their strengths and weaknesses. These systems can adapt the content and pace of instruction to meet each student's individual needs.

However, teachers play a crucial role in this process. They bring empathy, understanding, and the ability to motivate students in ways that AI simply cannot. By working together, AI can assist teachers in identifying areas where students may need extra help, allowing them to provide targeted support, as I explained in the above section, with a student finding it hard to balance between his study and sporting activity.

Human-AI collaboration has the potential to revolutionize problem-solving across multiple fields. By leveraging the strengths of both humans and AI, we can discover insights, drive innovation, and create better outcomes.

Recap

This chapter focuses on how AI can be a valuable tool for managing conflicts and complex issues, helping users develop strong problem-solving strategies. While conflict is challenging, AI can offer guidance, suggest steps, and even simulate multiple perspectives to provide comprehensive solutions.

We have also highlighted that, despite AI's assistance, users remain in control of the decision-making process and should treat AI's advice as a supportive resource. For added perspective, I encourage users to seek feedback on AI-generated solutions from trusted individuals.

A key technique introduced here is "AI Personas," which allows the AI to take on different expert roles, like a teacher, coach, or business executive. This multi-perspective approach helps users gain varied insights on challenges, providing a well-rounded problem-solving experience.

Finally, the chapter covers how human-AI collaboration can help in fields like healthcare, business, and education by combining human intuition with AI's data-processing power to tackle complex problems effectively.

Activity: Multi-Persona Problem-Solving

1. **Choose a Scenario**: Pick a problem, like planning a school event or improving team collaboration.
2. **Define Personas**: For example, a project manager, a team lead, and a designer.
3. **Initiate a Dialogue**: Use the prompt below to start the conversation:
   Prompt: "You are three people working on an event: Alex the project manager, Jamie the team lead, and Taylor the designer. Discuss how to organize the event for success and outline next steps."

Chapter 6

Creating Custom AI Agents

So, I want to close out this book with a tool that will catapult your routine processes to a different level. This technology is called AI Agents. Hang in there with me as I do my best to explain AI agents. In layman's terms, they are computer programs that can perform tasks or make decisions on their own, much like a virtual assistant. They use artificial intelligence to understand what you want and carry out actions based on that. Here are a few examples you would know and possibly interact with on a weekly, if not daily, basis:

Virtual Assistants: Think of Siri or Alexa. These AI agents can answer questions, play music, set reminders, and control smart home devices just by listening to your voice.

Chatbots: When you visit a website and see a little chat window pop up asking if you need help, that's a chatbot. It can answer your questions or guide you through the website.

Recommendation Systems: When you watch movies on Netflix, it suggests other movies you might like based on what you've watched before. This is an AI agent analyzing your preferences.

Autonomous Vehicles: Self-driving cars use AI agents to navigate roads, avoid obstacles, and make driving decisions without human help.

In ChatGPT, these agents are called Custom GPTs, and in Gemini, they're called Gems. Other platforms, like automation tools such as Zapier, have their own versions of these agents. But for the sake of this discussion, we'll focus on Custom GPTs, although you can use the same prompt-building process across most platforms.

Custom GPTs: A simplified version of an agent like custom GPTs allows you to create your own AI assistant that understands specific topics or tasks you want help with. For example, if you want an AI that helps you with math homework, you can customize it to focus on math problems and explanations. It's like having your personal tutor available whenever you need it!

At the end of the day, it's really dope how OpenSi has laid this thing out to allow everyday people to come up with pretty sweet agents. If you think of AI as your executive assistant from a 30,000-foot view, think about agents as individuals or separate entities that work within the AI realm. These agents are doing your bidding; they're experts in certain things. Yes, **you can create prompts to make temporary**

experts, but you can create custom agents to be experts and then do stuff.

To make sure you get the best output from these agents, you go back to **REACT**, which, of course, stands for Role, Example, Action, Context, Tone, and we will add **Output**. Think of custom GPTs as long prompts that are always there for you, but you can make them so that you can share them with others.

Practical Application: The Lightbulb Moment

For me, this was when the light came on.... I was like, this is an amazing tool. I see that I can actually use this. I see how it will become my executive assistant. But when I learned how easy it was to create my own agent, things started to come alive in my ministry and business. To the point now that the organizations I lead are "AI-first organizations". This means I'm literarily hiring people based on their ability to adjust because we have custom agents who work with us to get things done.

Let's roll the tape back a little bit and give a practical, real-life use case that we've done. I'm working with a group of pastors in the inner city through a program called the **Thrive Initiative**.

This whole program is designed to help urban pastors come together to learn several things and gain resources to be more effective in their communities. We've taken these leaders through a process where they collectively agree that they're going to reach youth and young adults in their communities. Once they decide to do that, it becomes their primary objective and what they're going to go after in the coming months.

I've walked them through a process from another book that I wrote called **"Doin' the MOST,"** which stands for Mission, Objective, Strategy, and Tactics. I walked them through the process of developing an action plan. In the middle of that process, I realized I was talking and going in and out talking about AI and all this stuff. And I realized, like, yo, I gotta help them understand what AI is.

Custom GPTs allows you to create your own AI assistant that understands specific topics or tasks you want help with.

So what I did was I taught them the MOST principle, which taught them how to do a simple action plan. And then, we took the next two sessions and started to create plans on paper.

I ended up building a custom agent for them using the MOST principle that they had learned two sessions prior. When they scanned a QR code, it took them to my custom agent. They go into it, and then they click on it. Then, the first thing is it asks them their name, what the name of the church is, and some other contact and context stuff.

One of the questions it asked them was: "What type of organization do you have? Tell me a little bit about yourself." So, it allows the agent to learn a little bit about the person and their context. From there, it'll start to frame the questions that it asks. I'll get to exactly how this works on the back end in a minute. But then it asks them a series of questions.

Now, I typically develop my agents so that they won't take a person longer than 20 minutes. Because I'm promoting that AI can save you significant time. If you have an agent, you have an executive assistant; you have helpers to execute. With these helpers, you can get through things that would typically take two hours and cut them down drastically, and literally, within 20 minutes, come up with a very comprehensive action plan. They would answer these questions, and at the end of it, the agent would produce them with a very nice plan based on their Mission, Objective, Strategy, and Tactics.

And what's dope is what happens when you see the light come on in a man who's 75 years old, who has never messed with AI and starts to see the idea that he owns, that he's in the driver's seat, that he gives to an assistant, and then the assistant gives it to the agents. And those agents run around in the background and start producing great stuff for this leader.

Behind the Scenes: Creating the Custom GPT

Basically, you go into a word processor to start creating your prompt. Please note this is a very long, specific prompt. This particular prompt is one that you are going to make once and use many times in the future. So you should take 30 minutes or so to do it if you have to.

Create a Custom GPT Using the REACTO Framework

Scenario: Strategic Planning Assistant for Non-Profit Organizations

Imagine you want to create a custom GPT that serves as a Strategic Planning Assistant specifically tailored for non-profit organizations. This assistant will help leaders develop comprehensive strategic plans using the MOST framework (Mission, Objective, Strategy, Tactics).

Applying the REACTO Framework

1. Role

Define the Role: Clearly specify the expertise and persona you want the AI to embody.

Prompt Example:

"You are the greatest strategic planning expert of all time, specializing in non-profit organizations. Your extensive experience and deep understanding of the MOST framework enable you to guide leaders in developing effective strategic plans."

2. Example

Provide Examples: Offer relevant examples, frameworks, or templates to guide the AI's responses.

Prompt Example:

"Here is a sample strategic plan template used by successful non-profits focusing on community outreach and engagement. Refer to this template to structure your responses."

Alternatively, if you have specific questions you want the GPT to ask, you can provide them:

"I have attached a document containing exact questions I want you to ask users to help them develop their strategic plans."

If attaching a document:

"I have attached a document(S) in the Knowledge section. Be sure to refer to it to understand the types of questions and frameworks you should utilize."

3. Action

Specify the Action: Clearly state the tasks or objectives you want the AI to accomplish.

Prompt Example:

"I want you to take the information from the attached document and ask a series of questions that will help users develop a strategic plan based on the MOST framework. After gathering the necessary information, produce a detailed strategic plan outlining Mission, Objectives, Strategies, and Tactics."

4. Context

Set the Context: Provide relevant background information to ensure the AI understands the environment and needs of the users.

Prompt Example:

"This assistant is intended for leaders of non-profit organizations who aim to improve their community impact. The users may range from new leaders seeking guidance to experienced managers looking to refine their strategic plans. Ensure that your questions and suggestions are tailored to help them achieve their life, work, career, or ministry goals."

5. Tone

Determine the Tone: Specify the desired language style, mood, and level of formality.

Prompt Example:

"Maintain a professional yet encouraging and inspirational tone throughout your interactions. Your responses should be clear, supportive, and motivating to help users feel confident in developing their strategic plans."

6. Output

Define the Output: Specify the format, structure, and any particular requirements for the final deliverable.

Prompt Example:

"Provide the strategic plan in a structured format with bullet points under each section of the MOST framework. Ensure that each section is clearly labeled and easy to follow. The entire plan should be concise yet comprehensive, fitting within a standard report length."

Putting It All Together: Full Instruction Set

Combining all elements of the REACTO framework, here's how your complete instruction set for the custom GPT might look:

Role:

"You are the greatest strategic planning expert of all time, specializing in non-profit organizations. Your extensive experience and deep understanding of the MOST framework enable you to guide leaders in developing effective strategic plans."

Example:

"Here is a sample strategic plan template used by successful non-profits focusing on community outreach and engagement. Refer to this template to structure your responses."

Action:

"I want you to take the information from the attached document and ask a series of questions that will help users develop a strategic plan based on the MOST framework. After gathering the necessary information, produce a detailed strategic plan outlining Mission, Objectives, Strategies, and Tactics."

Context:

"This assistant is intended for leaders of non-profit organizations who aim to improve their community impact. The users may range from new leaders seeking guidance to experienced managers looking to refine their strategic plans. Ensure that your questions and suggestions are tailored to help them achieve their life, work, career, or ministry goals."

Tone:

"Maintain a professional yet encouraging and inspiration tone throughout your interactions. Your responses should be clear, supportive, and motivating to help users feel confident in developing their strategic plans."

Output:

"Provide the strategic plan in a structured format with bullet points under each section of the MOST framework. Ensure that each section is clearly labeled and easy to follow. The entire plan should be concise yet comprehensive, fitting within a standard report length."

Then, after you test and tweak it, you simply make it shareable and share it!

Organizational Use of Custom Agents

I'm going through our systems and the processes that we use on a regular basis and asking the golden question: **"Can AI help me with this?"** For instance, we do behavioral and participant assessments, so I'm taking the assessments that we do with our leaders and building a custom GPT.

Then, they copy and paste their results and send them to me. And now there's an option where we can have it create automation through a platform called **Zapier**. We use that to make connections so that it will automatically email to us or drop into a spreadsheet.

I have created one agent, and I am really excited about **Troy Evans' Virtual Coach**. I uploaded everything that I know into this agent in the knowledge section. I've loaded my books, sermon notes, and all kinds of stuff so that it knows who I am, how I talk, and how I answer questions.

It's key that you try to organize your knowledge documents as best as possible and give them headers so that it will be easier for the AI to find the information. I put about ten PDFs in there so far, and I'll continue to add things to my "AI brain." When people interact with it, it kind of talks like me; it uses my terminology and my acronyms. Once it's loaded, a person can say, "What's up?" and ask your AI any questions.

Think about how powerful that can be when you have someone that you're coaching or someone who would like you to coach them and mentor them. But you can't do that with everybody. But you can send them to your virtual coach to help them on their journey.

Using Agents as Knowledge Bases

You can use custom agents as a knowledge base for team members. Individuals within your organization can ask questions about organizational policies, SOPs, and all your systems-based things. They will begin to go to AI first when you train your team to ask the AI golden question: **"Can AI help me with it first?"**

Now, remember that the best way to protect yourself when it comes to any technology is to have good data in, and so you can have good data out. And in this case, **don't put anything in that you don't want to go out.**

Recap: Custom GPT Agent

Step 1: Define the Role (R)

- **Action**: Specify the AI's role.

- **Example**: "You are the greatest strategic planning expert of all time."

Step 2: Provide Examples (E)

- **Action**: Include examples to guide the AI.

- **Example**: "You have successfully developed strategic plans for non-profit organizations focusing on youth engagement."

Step 3: Specify the Action (A)

- **Action**: Clearly state what you want the AI to do.

- **Example**: "I want you to ask a series of questions that will help develop a strategic plan based on the MOST framework."

Step 4: Set the Context (C)

- **Action**: Provide background information.

- **Example**: "This is for urban pastors aiming to reach youth and young adults in their communities."

Step 5: Determine the Tone (T)

- **Action**: Choose the communication style.

- **Example**: "Use an encouraging and accessible tone suitable for community leaders."

Step 6: Define the Output (O)

- **Action**: Specify the format and length.

- **Example**: "Provide the strategic plan in a structured format with bullet points under each section of the MOST framework."

Step 7: Utilize Knowledge Bases (Optional)

- **Action**: Attach relevant documents or data.

- **Example**: "I have attached a document containing additional resources. Refer to it when necessary."

Step 8: Create and Test the Agent

- **Action**: Input the compiled prompt into the AI platform.

- **Example**: Use ChatGPT's custom instructions feature or a similar tool. Test the agent by running through it yourself.

Step 9: Share and Implement

- **Action**: Share the custom agent with your team or use it in your workflow.

- **Example**: Provide team members with access to collaborative projects.

Custom AI agents have the power to transform how we work, learn, and collaborate. By investing time in creating tailored AI agents using the R.E.A.C.T.O framework, you can unlock crazy efficiency and specialization. Remember, the key is to be intentional with your prompts and to continually refine your agents as your needs evolve.

Chapter 7

Common Misconceptions About AI

There is no way I will end this book without addressing the misconception about AI. There's no denying that artificial intelligence (AI) has become one of the most talked-about topics in recent years. From movies and media to the workplace and our daily lives, AI seems to be everywhere. Yet, with all this attention comes a lot of misunderstanding and misconceptions about what AI actually is and what it can do.

Often, people think of AI as either a magical solution to all our problems or as a dangerous technology set to replace humans altogether. In reality, AI is neither a perfect solution nor a threat to our existence. It's an extremely powerful tool that, when used responsibly, can bring about incredible benefits.

Let's go through some of the most common myths surrounding AI and clear up these misconceptions. By better understanding this tool, we can see its true potential without getting lost in the hype or fear.

Myth #1: AI Will Take Over All Jobs and Leave Everyone Unemployed

One of the most widespread myths about AI is that it will take over all human jobs, leaving people out of work. While it's true that AI and automation are changing the job market, the reality is much more complex. AI can handle repetitive, time-consuming tasks, which means people will have more time for higher-level, creative, or human-centered roles.

For example, AI can automate data entry and certain aspects of customer service, freeing up employees to focus on tasks that require complex problem-solving and personal interaction. But for people like me and others who are ready to embrace AI and use my REACTO framework, we will always be in jobs.

What's actually happening is that AI is creating new job opportunities while transforming old ones. There's a growing demand for people who can design, manage, and understand AI systems, meaning jobs like AI ethics consultants, data analysts, and machine learning engineers are on the rise. Instead of taking away jobs, AI is pushing us to learn new skills and think in new ways. Some studies predict that the jobs created by AI could eventually outnumber the ones it automates.

Myth #2: AI Can Think and Feel Like Humans

Another common misconception is that AI can think, feel, or even possess consciousness like a human being. AI might be able to understand language, recognize faces, or even play chess, but it doesn't actually "understand" or "experience" any of these things in the way humans do. AI operates based on algorithms and patterns. It can be programmed to recognize certain cues or respond in specific ways, but it lacks emotions, consciousness, and true understanding.

This misunderstanding likely stems from how AI is portrayed in movies and TV shows. Characters like robots that "feel" or "love" make for great storytelling but don't represent reality. While AI can mimic certain human behaviors or emotions, it does not actually experience them. AI systems don't have a personal perspective or self-awareness; they're simply following patterns set by data.

Myth #3: AI Is Only for Big Tech Companies

A lot of people believe that AI is only for large corporations with huge budgets, like Google, Facebook, or Amazon. While these companies invest heavily in AI research and development, AI is increasingly accessible to smaller businesses and individuals like you and me, thanks to open-source software and affordable AI tools like ChatGPT, Gemini, and the like. Today, even small businesses can use AI for things like managing customer relationships, automating marketing tasks, or analyzing social media engagement.

There are also many online resources and courses that allow anyone to learn the basics of AI. Platforms like Google's TensorFlow, Microsoft Azure, and Amazon Web Services (AWS) offer AI tools that businesses of all sizes can use to streamline their operations. This democratization of AI is actually helping smaller businesses compete with larger ones by making it possible to automate tasks that were once out of reach for them.

Myth #4: AI Can Solve Any Problem, Instantly

Some people view AI as a miracle solution that can instantly solve any problem we throw at it. The truth is, while AI is powerful, it's not a magic fix for every challenge. AI systems are limited by the data they're trained on and by the goals they're programmed to achieve. If an AI system hasn't seen enough diverse data or been given clear instructions, it might struggle with accuracy or make mistakes. AI also relies heavily on human input, from training data to ongoing oversight and improvements.

For example, in medical diagnosis, an AI system can help identify patterns in scans or medical records, but it still requires a doctor's expertise to interpret the results and decide on the best treatment plan. In other words, AI is a tool that helps us make better, faster decisions, but it doesn't replace human judgment or expertise.

Myth #5: AI Is Dangerous and Will Eventually Dominate Humanity

There's a popular fear that AI might "turn on" humanity and take over, as seen in science fiction like "The Terminator." In reality, AI lacks the motivation or desire to dominate; it's not self-aware or independently driven. The risks of AI don't come from AI itself but rather from how people choose to use it.

Yes, AI is powerful, it's not a magic fix for every challenge.

Of course, like any powerful technology, AI can be misused if not managed responsibly. For instance, AI-driven facial recognition could be used to invade privacy, and automated weapons could raise ethical concerns. However, these issues are related to human decisions regarding AI development and use, not AI's "intentions." With proper regulation, ethical considerations, and oversight, AI can be managed in ways that minimize risks and maximize benefits.

Myth #6: AI Will Make Humans Less Important or Necessary

Some people worry that as AI becomes more capable, humans will become less relevant or needed. The truth is AI is designed to support and enhance human capabilities, not replace them. AI can help us handle enormous amounts of data or carry out complex calculations, but it relies on human insight, creativity, and empathy to be meaningful and effective.

For example, AI might be able to assist in creating art or music, but it lacks the human touch, emotions, and unique experiences that define creativity. Likewise, in healthcare, while AI can assist with data analysis, it's doctors and nurses who provide compassionate care and make critical decisions. AI works best when it's combined with human skills, and as we move forward, it's more likely to strengthen our roles than to diminish them.

Myth #7: AI Is Too Complicated for Ordinary People to Understand

AI can sound intimidating, but at its core, AI is just a way of using computers to solve problems by learning from data. With basic training and resources, anyone can get an understanding of how AI works. You don't need to be a tech expert to understand the basics of AI or to use AI tools effectively.

Of course, I wasn't a tech expert some years back, but now I use it every day of my life. This book and many other platforms today offer beginner-friendly tutorials, courses, and explanations that help people understand AI in a simple, accessible way.

In fact, it's beneficial for everyone to have a basic understanding of AI since it plays a larger role in our daily lives. Learning about AI doesn't mean you have to become a programmer; it's more about understanding how the technology works and how it can make your life easy.

As we continue to develop and adopt AI, it's important to stay informed and avoid falling for myths that exaggerate its capabilities or dangers. AI is a powerful tool that can help us in countless ways, from improving healthcare to enhancing business efficiency.

By educating ourselves, approaching AI with a realistic view, and embracing the opportunities it brings, we can harness its potential to make our lives better. Instead of fearing AI or putting it on a pedestal, let's focus on using it as a tool that helps us reach our goals, improve our quality of life, and make a positive difference in the world.

Recap

In this Chapter, we clear up common myths surrounding AI, explaining its real potential and limitations. Many think AI is either a magical solution or a threat to jobs and humanity itself. But the truth is that AI is simply a powerful tool that supports human tasks when used responsibly. AI doesn't "think" or "feel" as humans do; it operates based on data and patterns, not emotions or intentions. Another misconception is that AI is only for big tech companies, yet today's AI tools are accessible to businesses of all sizes.

Contrary to fears, AI isn't a quick fix for every problem, it relies on quality data and clear instructions to work effectively. Finally, AI is here to enhance human skills, not replace them. With proper education, anyone can learn to use AI in ways that improve everyday tasks and make life easier.

Activity: Debunking AI Myths

1. **Choose a Myth**: Pick one AI myth, like "AI will take over all jobs."
2. **Research and Refute**: Use accessible AI tools, like ChatGPT, to learn and discuss why this myth isn't entirely accurate.
3. **Present the Facts**: Write a brief explanation or present a slide highlighting why this myth is misleading and how AI can actually help.

Recap

In this guide, we've looked at AI, its history and usefulness in our day to day activity. We've also explored how to elevate AI from a basic assistant to an executive assistant capable of managing complex projects, aiding in brainstorming innovative ideas, and providing strategic solutions that can impact your bottom line. We introduced the concept of **Chain of Thought Prompting (COT)** as a method of engaging in a back-and-forth dialogue with AI to refine and expand ideas step by step. We also discussed the power of using multiple personas in AI to simulate discussions and gain diverse perspectives. Finally, we took a deep dive into creating custom AI agents using the **REACTO** framework, highlighting practical applications and the transformative potential of these agents in organizational settings.

Conclusion

Moving from using AI as a basic assistant to an executive assistant is a significant shift in how we view and interact with this technology. When you start seeing AI not just as a helper but as a crucial partner and collaborator, you unlock its power to tackle complex tasks and bring new ideas to the table. With AI as a partner, you're not just assigning it small, routine tasks, you're inviting it into major projects and decision-making processes. Whether you're planning a fundraising event, solving complex problems, or building a knowledge base for your organization, AI stands ready to collaborate with you.

To get the most out of AI, it's important to be thoughtful about how you engage with it. Start by crafting clear, intentional prompts that align with your goals. As you interact with AI, you'll likely refine your approach, learning which types of instructions bring out its best capabilities. Asking yourself regularly, **"Can AI help me with this?"** opens up new ways to utilize it in different areas of your work and life. By keeping an open mind, you'll find that AI can add efficiency, offer insights you hadn't considered, and even introduce creative solutions that might have taken much longer to arrive at on your own.

As you integrate AI more fully, it can drive productivity and uncover growth opportunities. With

AI as your executive-level partner, you'll save time on routine work, freeing up energy for strategic thinking and creative exploration. This shift to viewing AI as an executive assistant means you're not just working faster; you're working smarter, pushing the boundaries of what you can achieve in both personal and professional settings.